MILITARY MACHINES

MILITARY TRUCKS

by Melissa Abramovitz

Consulting Editor: Gail Saunders-Smith, PhD

Consultant: Raymond L. Puffer, PhD
Historian, Ret.
Edwards Air Force Base History Office

CAPSTONE PRESS
a capstone imprint

Pebble Plus is published by Capstone Press,
1710 Roe Crest Drive, North Mankato, Minnesota 56003.
www.capstonepub.com

Books published by Capstone Press are manufactured with paper
containing at least 10 percent post-consumer waste.

Library of Congress Cataloging-in-Publication Data
Abramovitz, Melissa, 1954–
   Military trucks / by Melissa Abramovitz.
      p. cm—(Pebble plus. Military machines)
   Includes bibliographical references and index.
   Summary: "Simple text and full-color photographs describe various military trucks"—Provided by publisher.
   ISBN 978-1-4296-7570-3 (library binding)
   ISBN 978-1-4296-7886-5 (paperback)
   1. Military trucks—United States—Juvenile literature. I. Title.
   UG618.A27 2012
   623.7'474—dc23   2011021660

Editorial Credits
Erika L. Shores, editor; Kyle Grenz, designer; Kathy McColley, production specialist

Photo Credits
iStockphoto/Craig DeBourbon, 7, 13
U.S. Air Force photo by Master Sgt. Juan Valdes, 19
U.S. Army photo by Spc. Charles Gill, 9, Spc. John Crosby, 5, Spec. Shawn Cassatt, 15, Staff Sgt. Michael Bracken, 11
U.S. Marine Corps photo by Lance Cpl. Ryan B. Busse, 21, Sgt. Richard L. McCumber III, 17
U.S. Navy photo by MC1 Miguel Angel Contreras, cover

Artistic Effects
Shutterstock: Hitdelight

Note to Parents and Teachers

The Military Machines series supports national science standards related to science, technology,
and society. This book describes and illustrates military trucks. The images support early readers
in understanding the text. The repetition of words and phrases helps early readers learn new
words. This book also introduces early readers to subject-specific vocabulary words, which are
defined in the Glossary section. Early readers may need assistance to read some words and to
use the Table of Contents, Glossary, Read More, Internet Sites, and Index sections of the book.

Printed in the United States of America in North Mankato, Minnesota.
052012   006702R

Table of Contents

What Are Military Trucks?

Every day, the U.S. Armed Forces put military trucks to work. Some trucks are big enough to carry battle tanks. Other trucks are as small as SUVs.

RSIZE LOAD

The smallest U.S. military truck is a Humvee. At 15 feet (4.6 meters) long, it's about the length of three bathtubs.

More than 30 feet (9 meters) long, HEMTTs are the biggest military trucks. One HEMTT is the length of six bathtubs.

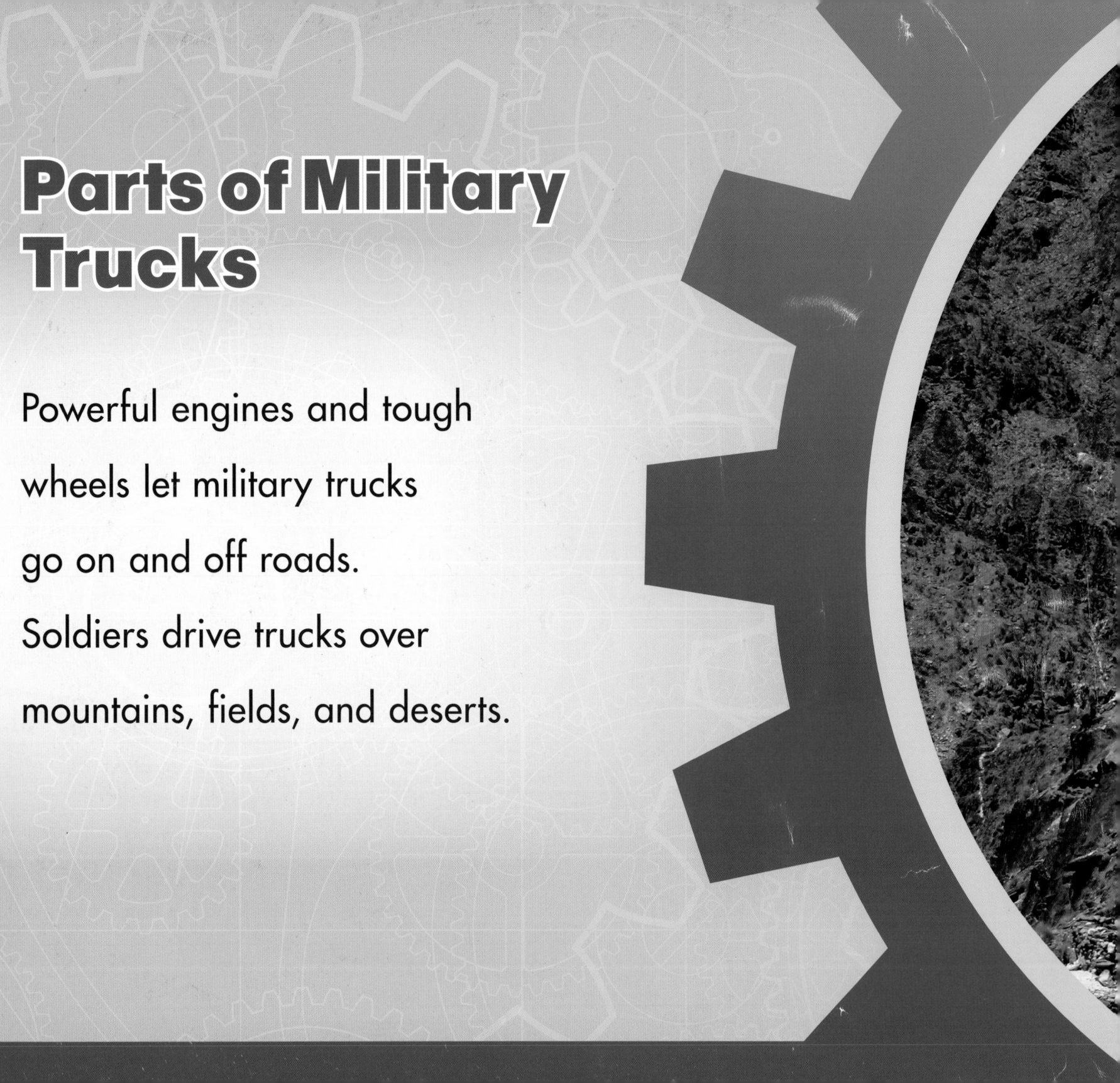

Parts of Military Trucks

Powerful engines and tough wheels let military trucks go on and off roads. Soldiers drive trucks over mountains, fields, and deserts.

The truck body holds soldiers or cargo. Armor covers MRAP vehicles to protect soldiers from guns and bombs.

Camouflage paint on a truck's body hides it from the enemy. Green paint blends in with trees. Tan paint blends in with sand.

Trucks in Action

Trucks take troops and supplies where the military needs them. LMTVs, MTVRs, and other trucks carry tons of cargo, including weapons, food, and tents.

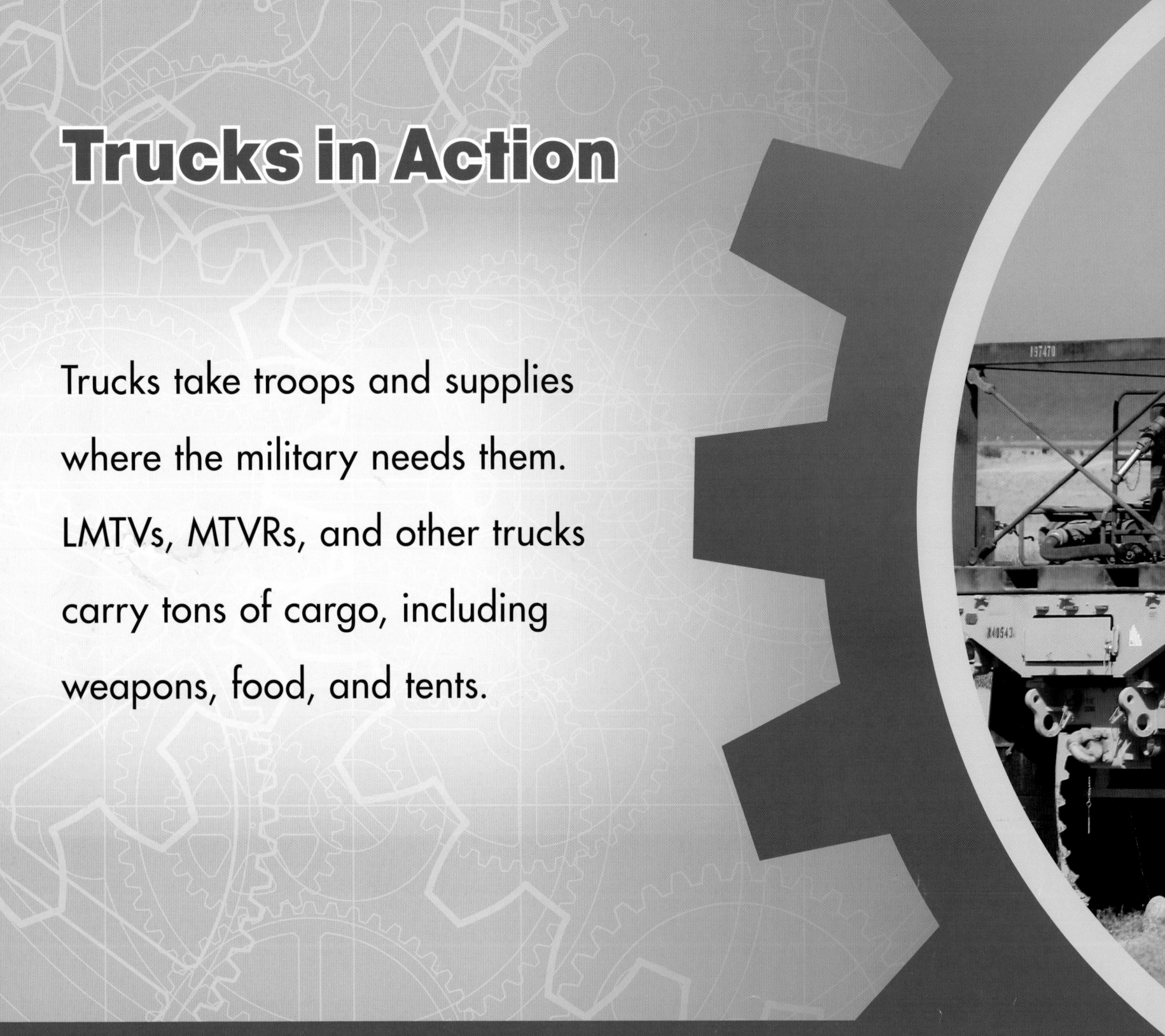

MTVR

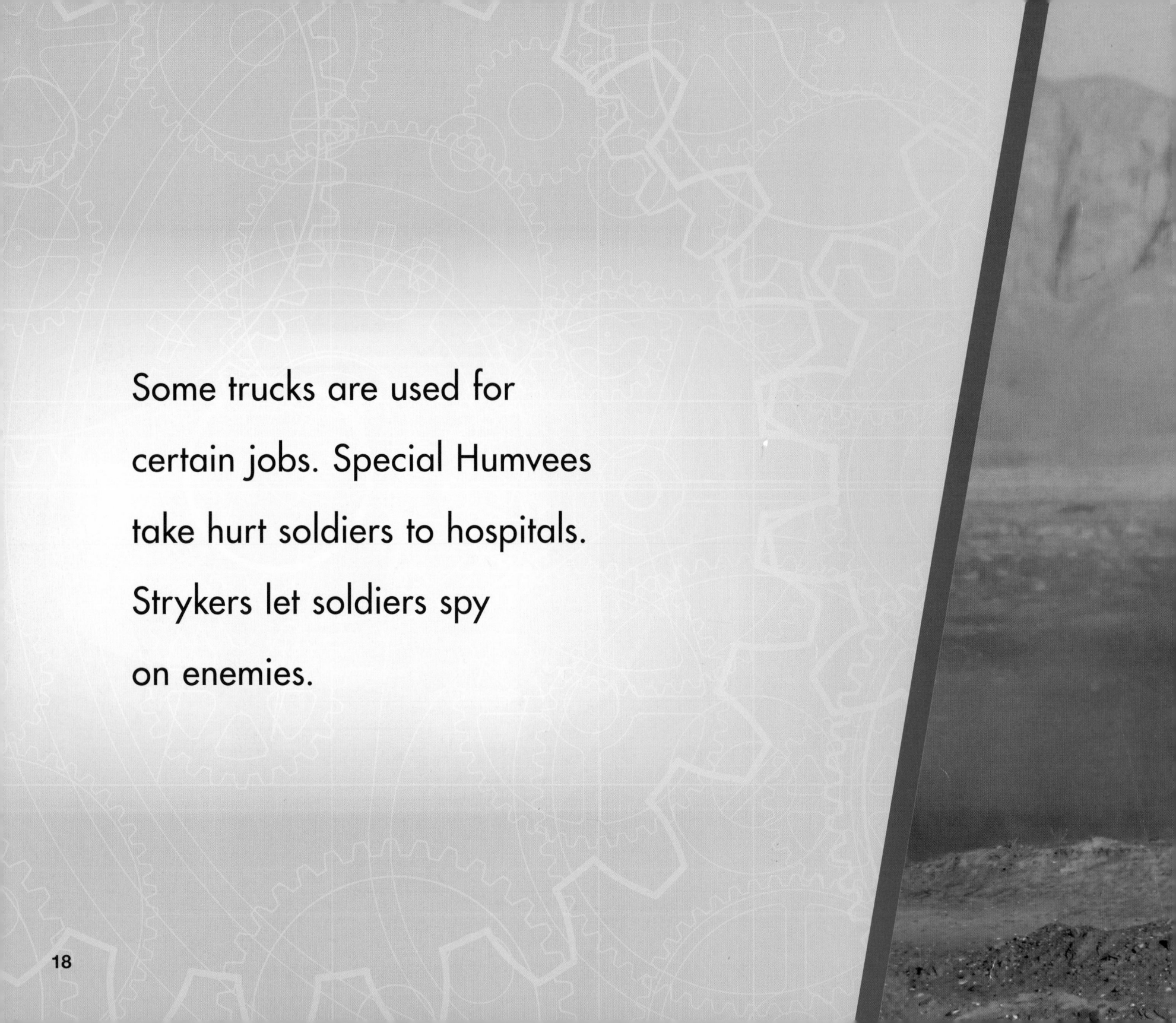

Some trucks are used for certain jobs. Special Humvees take hurt soldiers to hospitals. Strykers let soldiers spy on enemies.

Stryker

Military Machines

The military cannot fight wars
without tough, trusty trucks.
Day or night, rain or snow,
military trucks get the job done.

Glossary

Armed Forces—the whole military; the U.S. Armed Forces include the Army, Navy, Air Force, Marine Corps, and Coast Guard

armor—a protective metal covering

camouflage—a coloring or pattern that makes animals, people, or objects look like their surroundings

cargo—the goods carried by a vehicle

HEMTT—stands for Heavy Expanded Mobility Tactical Truck

LMTV—stands for Light Medium Tactical Vehicle

MRAP—stands for Mine Resistant Ambush Protected vehicle

MTVR—stands for Medium Tactical Vehicle Replacement

SUV—stands for sport utility vehicle

Read More

Doeden, Matt. *The U.S. Army.* Military Branches. Mankato, Minn.: Capstone Press, 2009.

Graham, Ian. *Military Vehicles.* Designed for Success. Chicago: Heinemann Library, 2008.

Hamilton, John. *Humvees.* Edina, Minn.: ABDO Pub. Co., 2011.

Internet Sites

FactHound offers a safe, fun way to find Internet sites related to this book. All of the sites on FactHound have been researched by our staff.

Here's all you do:

Visit *www.facthound.com*

Type in this code: 9781429675703

Check out projects, games and lots more at
www.capstonekids.com

Index

Word Count: 196
Grade: 1
Early-Intervention Level: 21